Silences from the Spanish Civil War

Jane Duran

Silences from the Spanish Civil War

ENITHARMON PRESS

2002

First published in 2002
by the Enitharmon Press
26B Caversham Road
London NW5 2DU

www.enitharmon.co.uk

Distributed in the USA and Canada
by Dufour Editions Inc.
PO Box 7, Chester Springs
PA 19425, USA

ISBN 1 900564 67 X

British Library Cataloguing in Publication Data.
A catalogue record for this book is available
from the British Library.

Typeset in Bembo by Servis Filmsetting Ltd
and printed in England by
The Cromwell Press

ACKNOWLEDGEMENTS

I am grateful to the Arts Council for a Writer's Award (1998), and to the MacDowell Colony in Peterborough, New Hampshire for their fellowship in 2000 while this work was in progress.

'Battle of Teruel, Winter 1937-38' was published in *La Generación del Cordero* (Trilce Ediciones, 2000); and 'Spanish Peasant Boy' and 'The Pyrenees' appeared in *Parents: An Anthology of Poems by Women Writers* (Enitharmon Press, 2000).

My thanks to Kamal Ayyildiz, Heather Birrell, Cheli Durán, Rhian Gallagher, Gloria García Lorca, Mimi Khalvati and Pedro Serrano for reading drafts of the sequence at various stages and for their valuable comments; and to Ricardo Sola Buil and Alfonso Casas Ologaray for introducing me to areas in Aragón where the Civil War was fought.

I am grateful to all those who generously shared their knowledge or experience of the Spanish Civil War and its aftermath with me. Among these are Francisco Ferrer Gasulla, Jesús Gómez Vera, Lala Isla, José Lamiel, David Mitchell, Joaquim Puig Ferrer, Aniceto Rallo Gasulla, Sam Russell, Javier Sanz Faure, Josep Saumell Fonoll, Tomás Segovia and Manuel Vegas Asín.

And to my husband Redha, my thanks for his encouragement and support while I was writing this book.

Jane Duran

CONTENTS

These poems are dedicated to the memory of my father, Gustavo Durán, who fought in the Spanish Civil War with the Republican Army between 1936 and 1939. He was born in Barcelona in 1906. He played the piano from an early age and studied music at the Real Conservatorio de Música in Madrid, and later in Paris. As a student and composer, he became close to a group of artists, writers and composers at the Residencia de Estudiantes, particularly Federico García Lorca, Rafael Alberti and Luis Buñuel.

On 18 July 1936, the first day of the war, my father joined the Republican Army, serving on an armoured train with railroad workers. Soon he was asked to organise a motorised battalion, and early in 1937 he formed the 69th Mixed Brigade. This brigade fought at Jarama, Guadalajara and Madrid, and at La Granja in the Segovia offensive. My father also worked closely with the Alianza de Intelectuales Antifascistas to enlist support for the Republican cause through the arts.

In the summer of 1937 my father received orders to form the 47th Division. This division took part in the battles of Brunete and Teruel. After the Nationalists recaptured Teruel, they launched an offensive through Aragón and the Republicans were forced to retreat through the Sierra del Maestrazgo, where my father formed the Mountain Group from the remnants of his division and other army units. When they reached the coast, this group split in two. My father retained command of the Coastal Group which went south to help protect Valencia. In May 1938 he was promoted to the rank of Lieutenant-Colonel and given command of the 20th Army Corps of the Levante.

At the end of the war my father escaped from the port of Gandía aboard a British naval ship. He never returned to Spain. In England he met and married my mother, Bonté Crompton, an American. Together they lived in the United States, Cuba, Chile and finally Greece. He died in Athens in 1969 and was buried in Crete.

I have tried to listen to my father's silence about the Spanish Civil War and what it might be saying. The poems began as an effort to catch glimpses of that experience, which changed the course of his life. In the process, I was drawn into the events and issues of the war through historical books, eyewitness accounts and photographs that documented its early hopes and long and painful unfolding.

As the scope of the sequence widened, I thought it would be helpful to include a summary of the causes and decisive moments of the war. I am immensely grateful to Paul Preston for his illuminating introduction, which covers some of the events and circumstances touched on in the poems.

The Spanish Civil War was essentially the struggle of Franco and his foreign allies to destroy the Second Republic, the democratic regime supported by a majority of the Spanish people. The departure for exile of King Alfonso XIII on 14 April 1931 had been greeted with scenes of popular rejoicing in most of Spain's large towns. Those who danced in the streets hoped that the new democracy would introduce a sweeping programme of social reforms to improve the lot of both the industrial working class and the huge mass of landless labourers who worked the great estates of the south in conditions of such poverty as to make their plight almost indistinguishable from slavery. Unfortunately, the Republic's room for manoeuvre was severely limited. It was established in the midst of the great depression, and the harsh weather conditions of the winter of 1930-1931 saw widespread harvest failure. For the first two years of the Second Republic in Spain, between 1931 and 1933, a coalition of moderate Socialists and middle class liberal Republicans attempted to implement their programme of social reform at the same time as trying to break the power of two great pillars of the old regime – the Catholic Church and the Army. Special loans were taken out to make possible a plan for the creation of 27,000 new schoolrooms and the teachers to run them. Many intellectuals took part in the so-called *misiones pedagógicas* (teaching missions), which took literacy classes, mobile libraries, and popular theatre to the most remote villages of rural Spain. They were appalled to find that physical hunger often accompanied a hunger for culture. As the dramatist Alejandro Casona commented, 'they needed bread and medicine and we had only songs and poems in our bags'.

Although the Republican project was fundamentally moderate, the press and radio networks of the right vilified these attempts to modernise Spain as assaults on cherished traditional values. The success of right-wing resistance to reform led to divisions within the ruling coalition. Disillusioned with the slowness of reform, the Socialists decided to fight the November 1933 elections alone in the hope of establishing an exclusively Socialist government that would pursue change more robustly. In a system which favoured coalitions, this was a tactical error that handed victory to a group of right-wing parties. Throughout 1934, that rightist coalition overturned the minimal social and religious reforms of 1931-1933. Wages were slashed and trade unionists persecuted. Fearful that the Right planned to establish a fascist state, in October Socialists, anarchists and Communists rose up in the northern mining districts of Asturias only to be defeated by units of the ferocious Spanish Foreign Legion. The repression was put under the supervision of General Francisco Franco. It was the first battle of the Civil War. The Right took its revenge with considerable savagery. The left-wing press was silenced, unions were closed down and nearly 30,000 leftists were imprisoned. The Left was impelled to reunite in the Popular Front. In the February 1936 elections, the Popular Front won a narrow victory and immediately began to revive the reforming programme of 1931. Alarmed by the new-found confidence of the Left, the Right prepared for war. A military conspiracy was hatched under the leadership of General Emilio Mola. The growing fascist party, Falange Española, used terror squads to create the disorder to justify the imposition of an authoritarian regime. The Left's response to terrorist attacks contributed to the spiral of violence. The assassination on 13 July of the monarchist leader, José Calvo Sotelo, provided convenient justification for the conspirators.

The plotters had not foreseen a long civil war. The generals' rising succeeded in the provincial capitals of rural León and Old Castile, towns like Burgos, Salamanca and Avila, but was defeated by the workers in Madrid, Barcelona and the industrial cities of the North. In the South, the countryside fell to the Left but, in the major towns like Cádiz, Seville and Granada, working-class resistance was savagely eliminated. The rebels controlled one third of Spain in a huge block including Galicia, León, Old Castile, Aragón and part of Extremadura and an Andalusian triangle from Huelva to Seville to Córdoba. They had the great wheat-growing areas, but the main industrial centres remained in Republican hands. There, the military coup led to the total collapse of the apparatus of the state. The subsequent vacuum of authority made possible a remarkable social experiment. The fight against fascism was seen by many on the left as an opportunity to build a new egalitarian world to replace the social injustice that characterised Spain's towns and countryside. In the event, the demands of the war effort would provoke internecine conflict over whether priority should be given to making the revolution or defeating the rebels and thus prevent the full flowering of the industrial and agrarian collectives of the Republican zone. Nevertheless, the way in which the Spanish working class faced the dual tasks of war against the old order and of construction of the new, lies at the heart of the enduring interest in the Spanish Civil War. George Orwell acknowledged this: 'I recognized it immediately as a state of affairs worth fighting for'. The anarchist leader, Buenaventura Durruti, expressed what was at stake when he told a reporter, 'We are not afraid of ruins, we are going to inherit the earth. The bourgeoisie may blast and ruin their world before they leave the stage of history. But we carry a new world in our hearts.'

While the left in the Republican zone attempted to build a new world, the right in the rebel zone immediately began to shore up the old order. Extremists in both zones set about eliminating class enemies with appalling savagery. Hatred on both sides soon escalated, in large part as a response to news of atrocities. In areas controlled by the military rebels, who took the name of Nationalists, there were mass 'trials', often lasting only a few minutes, of those associated with left-wing and liberal parties. In addition to the 'legal' executions that followed them, there were also large numbers of killings with no pretence of legality. These were called *paseos*, the victims being 'taken for a ride' and their corpses left at the sides of roads or dumped in cemeteries. Perhaps the most notorious of such assassinations was that of the Andalusian poet, Federico García Lorca on 19 August 1936. In ultra-reactionary Granada, his homosexuality had given him a sense of apartness and a sympathy for those on the margins of respectable society. His openly declared commitment to the left – 'I will always be on the side of those who have nothing', he said – had seen him set up the itinerant theatre *La Barraca*. Such murders were usually carried out by Falangists and sanctioned by the Nationalist authorities who claimed to be fighting in defence of Christian civilisation. They went on long after the Civil War had ended. In the Republican or 'loyalist' zone too, there were killings of middle- and upper-class individuals and of Catholic clergy, usually at the hands of criminal elements or anarchist fanatics. The Republican government made massive efforts to re-establish the authority of the state. Law and order was a major priority and, by early 1937, the atrocities came to an end in the areas controlled by the Republic. In the rebel zone during the war, and in Franco's Spain thereafter, extermination of the left-wing and liberal enemy was a deliberate act of policy.

Nevertheless, the bloodletting was the work of a significant minority on both sides, but a minority nonetheless. The bloody excesses of extremists were not something which, despite many enduring myths, involved all of those who took part in, or were affected by, the Spanish Civil War. In the Republican zone, there were those who were fighting merely for the preservation of democracy, others for particular anarchist, Communist or Socialist visions of the future. In the rebel zone, there were those who were fighting to bring back the monarchy, to defend the Catholic Church or to protect property. However, many Spaniards in both zones regarded the war with horror and were dragged into it with fear and repugnance. For those caught in the 'wrong' zone, to avoid execution or assassination, they had to feign what has been called 'geographical loyalty'. In consequence, the armed forces of both sides faced the problem of desertions as men tried to make it to the zone that best represented their beliefs.

In the immediate aftermath of the coup, the rebels confronted unexpected initial problems. In the major towns, weapons had been distributed to members of left-wing parties and trade unions who rapidly formed militia units. Although completely untrained, they set off enthusiastically to fight the rebels at the nearest front. The militias of Barcelona, made up of anarchists and of the anti-Stalinist communists of the Partido Obrero de Unificación Marxista, the POUM, went to recapture Zaragoza. As they poured into Aragón, they collectivised the land. The columns sent by Mola against Madrid were halted at the Sierra to the north by Socialist and Communist militias. In the early days of the war, women too joined the militias and bore arms, although the Republican government endeavoured to keep them away from the front. The rebels' strongest card was the so-called Army of Africa. Consisting of the brutal Spanish Foreign Legion and the Moroccan mercenaries of the Regulares Indígenas (Native Regulars), it was a battle-hardened force with long experience of terrorising civilians during Spain's colonial wars. Commanded by General Franco, it was blockaded in Morocco by Republican warships whose crews had mutinied against their rightist officers. Accordingly, they turned abroad for help. Enticed by the possibility of causing problems for the French, Hitler and Mussolini separately decided to provide the transport aircraft that, in early August, would make possible a major airlift from Morocco to Seville. Fifteen thousand men crossed in ten days and a *coup d'état* going wrong became a long and bloody civil war. The Republic, in contrast, was abandoned by the democratic powers. Inhibited by internal political divisions and by British fear of provoking a general war, the French premier Léon Blum soon drew back from early promises to aid the Republic, which was forced to turn to the Soviet Union.

The Nationalist rebels now undertook two campaigns which dramatically improved their situation. Mola attacked the Basque province of Guipúzcoa, cutting it off from France. Meanwhile, Franco's Army of Africa advanced rapidly northwards to Madrid, leaving an horrific trail of slaughter in its wake, including the massacre at Badajoz where 2,000 prisoners were shot. By 10 August, they had joined the two halves of Nationalist Spain. The rebels consolidated their position considerably throughout August and September. General José Enrique Varela connected up Seville, Córdoba, Granada and Cádiz. For the Republicans, there were no such spectacular advances. The rebel garrison of Toledo was still under siege in the fortress of the Alcázar and the anarchist militia columns from Barcelona were to be engaged for eighteen months in a futile attempt to recapture Zaragoza which had fallen quickly to the rebels.

On 21 September at an airfield near Salamanca, the leading rebel generals met to choose a commander-in-chief both for obvious military reasons and to facilitate relations with Hitler and Mussolini. Franco was chosen as single commander. On the same day, he decided to divert his columns, now at the gates of Madrid, to the South East to relieve the Alcázar of Toledo. He thus lost an unrepeatable chance to sweep onto the capital before its defences were ready. However, he was able to clinch his own power with an emotional victory and a great journalistic coup. He was also concerned to slow down the pace of the war in order to be able to carry out a thorough political purge of captured territory. On 28 September, Franco was confirmed as Head of the Nationalist State. Thereafter, he ruled over a tightly centralised zone. In contrast, the Republic was already severely hampered by intense divisions between the Communists and moderate Socialists who wanted to make a priority of the war effort and the anarchists, Trotskyists and left Socialists who wanted to put the emphasis on social revolution.

On 7 October the Army of Africa resumed its march on a Madrid inundated with refugees and beset by major supply problems. Franco's delay permitted the morale of the defenders of Madrid to be boosted by the arrival of arms from the Soviet Union and the columns of volunteers known as the International Brigades. For Italian, German and Austrian refugees from fascism and Nazism, Spain was the first real chance to fight back and, if they could defeat fascism, eventually to return to their homes. Volunteers from France, the Unites States, Britain and countries across the world made the hazardous journey to Spain believing that victory for the Spanish Republic was the only way to stop fascism and a future world war. They faced enormous difficulties – distance, official harassment and personal sacrifices – to fight for the Republic. Most were working class, some unemployed, others were intellectuals, a few adventurers, but all had come prepared to die in the fight against fascism. They arrived in Spain in October and were trained at Albacete. Organised under the auspices of the Comintern in the late summer and early autumn of 1936, the International Brigades included many volunteers who were not Communists. Their arrival made a difference but the siege of Madrid saw an heroic effort by the entire population. Nevertheless, on 6 November the government fled to Valencia, leaving the capital in the hands of General José Miaja. Backed by the Communist-dominated Junta de Defensa, he rallied the population while his brilliant Chief of Staff, Colonel Vicente Rojo, organised the city's forces. Despite the assistance of the crack German specialised units known as the Condor Legion, by late November Franco acknowledged the failure of his assault. The besieged capital would hold out for another two and a half years.

Franco's immediate response was a series of attempts to encircle the capital. At the battles of Boadilla (December 1936), Jarama (February 1937) and Guadalajara (March 1937), his forces were beaten back at enormous cost to the Republic. Even after the defeat of Guadalajara, in which a large contingent of Italian troops were involved, the Nationalists held the initiative. This was demonstrated by the ease with which they captured northern Spain in the Spring and Summer of 1937. In March, Mola led 40,000 troops in an assault on the Basque Country backed by terror-bombing expertise of the Condor Legion. The most extreme example was the annihilation of Guernica on 26 April 1937 to shatter Basque morale and undermine the defence of the capital, Bilbao, which fell on 19 June. For many, the Spanish Civil War is symbolised by the bombing of Guernica which has given rise to as much impassioned polemic as any incident in the Second World War. That is less because of the power of Picasso's painting than because Guernica saw the *first* extensive destruction of an undefended civilian target by aerial bombardment. Guernica was part of a trial run of the ground-air coordination techniques that underlay the *Blitzkrieg*. Newsreel pictures of the damage done by German and Italian bombing raids on Madrid and Barcelona and of civilians taking shelter in underground railway stations also helped to burn the Spanish Civil War into the European consciousness. Such images foreshadowed the new and horrific form of modern warfare that was to come. It was a reflection of the comparative resources of the two sides that most bombing during the war was carried out by German and Italian aircraft on behalf of Franco. The Republic had very few bombers and thus carried out only sporadic and ineffective night raids on Nationalist towns.

After the fall of the Basque Country, the Nationalist army, amply supplied with Italian troops and equipment, captured Santander on 26 August. Asturias was quickly mopped up during September and October. Northern industry was now at the service of the rebels. This gave them a decisive advantage to add to their numerical superiority in terms of men, tanks and aeroplanes.

Vicente Rojo tried to halt the Nationalists' inexorable process by a series of offensives. At Brunete, west of Madrid, on 6 July, 50,000 troops smashed through enemy lines, but the Nationalists had enough reinforcements to plug the gap. For ten days, in one of the bloodiest encounters of the war, the Republicans were pounded by air and artillery attacks. At enormous cost, the Republic slightly delayed the eventual collapse of the north. Then, in August 1937, Rojo made a bold pincer movement against Zaragoza. At the small town of Belchite, the offensive ground to a halt in mid-September. Belchite was reduced to rubble and, after 1939, its stark ruins were left as a monument to the war. As at Brunete, the Republicans gained an initial advantage, but lacked the force for the killer blow. In December 1937, Rojo launched a further pre-emptive attack against Teruel, in the hope of diverting Franco's latest assault on Madrid. The plan worked. In the most intense cold, the Republicans captured Teruel on 8 January but were dislodged after six weeks of heavy battering by artillery and bombers. After another costly defence of a small advance, the Republicans had to retreat on 21 February 1938, when Teruel was on the point of being encircled. The casualties on both sides had been enormous.

The Nationalists now consolidated their victory with a massive offensive through Aragón and Castellón towards the sea. 100,000 troops, 200 tanks and nearly 1,000 German and Italian aircraft began their advance on 7 March 1938. The Republicans were exhausted, short of guns and ammunition and demoralised after the defeat of Teruel. By early April, the rebels had reached Lérida and then moved down the Ebro valley, cutting off Catalonia from the rest of the Republic. The Republicans retreated painfully towards the coast through the harsh and arid hills of the Maestrazgo between Aragón and Castellón. By 15 April, the Nationalists had reached the Mediterranean at the fishing village of Vinaroz. In July, Franco launched a major attack on Valencia. The Nationalist Generals José Varela, Antonio Aranda and Rafael García Valiño found the southward progress difficult down through the rocky terrain of the Maestrazgo towards the coast. Brilliantly marshalled by General Leopoldo Menéndez López and Lieutenant-Colonel Gustavo Durán, the

Republicans defended with dogged determination ensuring that the Nationalists' progress was slow and exhausting. However, they came on inexorably. By 23 July 1938, Valencia was under direct threat, with the Nationalists less than forty kilometres away. In response, Rojo launched a spectacular diversion in the form of a great assault across the River Ebro in an attempt to restore contact with Catalonia. Crossing the river along a huge bend from from Flix in the north to Miravet in the south on the night of 24-25 July, the Republicans reached Gandesa nearly forty to fifty kilometres from their starting points but there they were bogged down as Nationalist reinforcements were rushed in. A desperate battle for the territory which had been taken lasted for over three months. Despite its strategic irrelevance, Franco was determined to smash the Republican army. By mid-November, at horrendous cost in casualties, the Republicans were pushed out of the territory captured in July. They left behind them many dead and much precious material.

Effectively, the Republic was defeated. Barcelona fell on 26 January 1939. Hundreds of thousands of terrified women, children, old men and defeated soldiers began to trek towards France. Through bitterly cold sleet and snow, on roads bombed and strafed by Nationalist aircraft, many walked, wrapped in blankets and clutching a few possessions, some carrying infants. Those who could squeezed into every kind of transport imaginable. From 28 January, a reluctant French Government allowed the first refugees across the border. The women, children and the old were shepherded into transit camps. Regarded as savages and murderers, the Republican soldiers were disarmed and escorted to insanitary camps on the coast, rapidly improvised by marking out sections of beach with barbed wire. The largest and most notorious were to be found on the beaches of southern France at Saint Cyprien, Argelès-sur-Mer and Barcarès. Lacking basic shelter or sanitary or cooking facilities, the living conditions were appalling. In the first six months after the end of the war, 14,672 Spaniards died from malnutrition, dysentery and bronchial illnesses. The retreat of the wretched human mass moving slowly north was covered by the desperate heroism of the remnants of the Republican army. In Madrid, on 4 March, the commander of the Republican Army of the Centre, Colonel Segismundo Casado revolted against the Republican government in the hope of stopping increasingly senseless slaughter. His hopes of a negotiated peace were rebuffed by Franco and, after a minor civil war within the civil war, troops all along the line began to surrender. The Nationalists entered an eerily silent Madrid on 27 March. Casado fled to Valencia where thousands of Republicans gathered vainly hoping to escape by sea. The Nationalist fifth column began to take over the city on 29 March and, on the following day, General Aranda arrived with the forces of occupation. In Valencia, Alicante, Gandía and other ports of the Levante coast, those who did not escape or commit suicide were herded into concentration camps.

Franco's dictatorship would be the institutionalisation of his victory. He had deliberately fought a slow war of attrition, with horrific purges in each piece of captured territory, as an investment in terror to underpin his future regime. By 31 March 1939, all of Spain was in Nationalist hands. About 350,000 people were killed in the course of the war. At least 50,000 people were shot by the Francoists between 1939 and 1943. Prisoners numbered nearly one million and some were forced into 'work battalions' to be used as cheap labour in the construction of dams, bridges and irrigation canals. The most infamous fruit of their labour was Franco's great mausoleum for the Nationalist war dead, the Valle de los Caídos near El Escorial. About 400,000 Republicans went into exile, most never to return. The emotional cost of exile for all of them was incalculable. Most also suffered considerable material privation. Only a small minority who had funds or skills secured a decent living, most often in Latin America. Others nearer Spain usually found themselves forced into the French Foreign Legion, German labour brigades or concentration camps. The need to learn new languages and find work in a hostile environment meant that most exiles had little time to devote to Spain. For those who stayed behind, fear was made a way of life. The population was demoralised. In town and country, informers abounded. Curfews and a system of safe-conducts were in force. Between 1939 and 1944, the so-called Ministry of Justice admitted to a figure of over 190,000 executed or died in prison. Many released from jail were seriously ill or else demoralised by the fear of being arrested again. Hunger and the virtual impossibility of getting work diminished the combative capacity of the Republicans. Conditions in working-class districts were appalling: people in rags searched for scraps, many lived in caves; there were no medical services.

In 1964, General Franco and his supporters were delighted by a noisy year-long celebration of the 'Twenty-Five Years of Peace' since the end of the Civil War. It began with a solemn Te Deum in the basilica at the Valle de los Caídos. The mass celebrated not peace but victory. Every town and village in Spain was bedecked with posters asserting that the Nationalist war effort had been a religious crusade to purge Spain of the atheistic hordes of the Left. For the Caudillo, the defeated were the '*canalla* (scum) of the Jewish-Masonic-Communist conspiracy' and the civil war 'the struggle of the *Patria* [the fatherland] against the *anti-Patria*, of national unity against separatism, of morality against iniquity, of the spirit against materialism.' One of his central post-war objectives had been to maintain a festering division of Spain between the victorious and the vanquished, the privileged 'authentic Spain' and the castigated 'anti-Spain'. For the defeated, Franco's peace meant the silence of the graveyard.

PAUL PRESTON
London School of Economics

There is a steep escarpment I lift myself onto
and a final shine where the rocks labour.
I am careful not to enter this land, to go inland.
The free waves take me only so far.

I know it is Spain, Spain all over again,
the place my father cannot go to
the place his friends in New York cannot go to,
his friends in Mexico, in Buenos Aires and Rome.
Pablo and Angel and Paco,
Laura and Pedro and Teresa.
They are kind, they embrace me.

I enter the war, resting the book on my knees.
The dense poplars gather around me,
the devastated villages.

He lays down his arms.
He raises his arms over his head.
He will not tell.

I can scarcely imagine it happened –
where it would be – the places of it.
Quiet places I visit now – torn up grass,
headed-off mist, depositions
of rose, vine, earth. Aragón all night
a cruel river you need to cross.
Here, and here, they say leading you
from the square, the church steps.
Here, by these houses, and on this hill
of fervent olive trees – yes, this very.

Research

A long gradient, the minute distances
to achieve the height, to even know
what I am searching for

like a mote in the eye, or a speck,
a belief, privations.
Then I am dangerously close

then I feel an exhaustion in all my limbs
the very moment
I hope to recover what is sincerely gone

and I look at my blistered hands
and feet, and think
it is this.

Maestrazgo

The deeper I go in the wind
the more unreal the days of departure
till I reach a look-out point
over distant farmhouses, sheepfolds

and see the waterline of the mountain range
as if it were part of me,
the friendliness and force it exerts on me.

My father said goodbye. He joined the militia.
Everything is lifted up and dries.
It is a long way down
from all parched things.

after a drawing by Benjamín Palencia

Perhaps you have sworn
to be still like this,
in your loud stone boots
your cropped hair
and sleeves too short
in a ploughed field,
the civil war
still far from your village.

You can hear it already
and pay attention.
It will come, one day,
right into the square
the sheep pass over
as my hand passes over
this paper, into the fastnesses
of doorways and sheepfolds.

Perhaps you will see my father
in the band of soldiers
with his hair cropped too,
the cypresses toiling
along the edge of your field.
Perhaps you will leave everything
as he did

and cross borders,
go to France, America,
anywhere that will have you.

Now that you have returned
what does the town say to you,
the Plaza de la República
and the bullring, the cemetery?

After so many years away,
so much event in your own life
what do you still remember
of the massacre?

Take us through it slowly
so it is almost retrieved –
the sweat on your brow.
1936, Badajoz. Tell us, stop,
try to compose yourself.

To the Aragón Front

I see, and then believe them —
fists raised, hanging, leaning from train
windows, those high spirits and embraces.
I want to argue with them.
I am clear about the news.

I have no place in this moment, but I live in it,
in those train windows, as I lived in the windows
of New York City, a long going-away
in the grip of them, for they are edging
forward and they will go, all those
defeats will occur like a wide swing
of the train, so measured, toppling the horizon,

they will occur as things must do
because they are in the past now.
But if I follow I will be with my father there.
I will know who he was and I will mourn with him.

The day calm, a jacket hung on a tree,
shadows bringing a wood-shack peace.
It might be Canada, it might be anywhere
where learning is happening in the open.

There is an eagerness about the way
they all lean in: a teacher, a blackboard
with a drawing, vertical lines, diagonals, dots.
They are eager to learn and maybe smiling,

sitting easily on the grass, arms round their knees,
in espadrilles or sandals. One rubs his eyes,
moves closer in. Those espadrilles – the ribbons
encircling, pressing into the soft flesh

and the white, loosened mariner's cloth
at toe and heel, up there in the hills, in the mild hills.

Paseos, 1936

It's the same road but darkened,
chilly or hidden –
like a maze I return to –
this straight road that crosses
the plain, that leaps across.

Each time it isn't me.
Each time the voices aren't there
to intervene
when the lorry arrives
in the 2's and 3's of the morning

and someone isn't shouting
and there is scuffling and a soft
pressure of light
from a neighbour's open door.

In the morning the village
will be exhausted and threadbare.
The road will be apparent now,
its perilous crossing in sunlight.
Each time it isn't me or mine.

LEGGINGS, 1936

When he moves away the child is trying
to tie them, the new leather leggings.
The child's hands are soft and small.

The man has a sword, a beard, a rifle,
he is ready for anything
but these leggings trouble him –

they will measure the dust behind him.
And the child, you see, doesn't let go.
He is fumbling at the laces, struggling

and the houses down the hillside
split in the first sunlight, split open.
The work of dressing so the man's life

can be taken away from the child,
the bad sun purposeful. The man has a purpose
and the child, being helpful, helps him

in his mission, so he is stopped
from moving away for a few moments.

GOATSKIN

This is how they gather in a room
pressed together over a map
what a hand feels like on a shoulder

what it is like to walk through mist
together and disappear
stepping down on mud, easy.

He holds up the goatskin
and wine streams out,
his mouth is open.

He hands the wine on.
And this is where he is not
where he is gone.

International Brigades

Arriving from Russia, Canada,
France, with banners, rifles
the avenues usher them along,
cobblestones, elms,

rain drying suddenly
on our faces.
A scratch in the photograph
links them, young, strong

coming to our rescue.
And we dance for them
we dance for them.

BELCHITE

We see Belchite from far away
so we can prepare ourselves for it.
It's exposed on the plain
and nothing can unsay it.

Why is it so necessary
to walk down the main street
and live out its emptiness?
What is rubble, ruin, sky to us?

How near can we come
in sympathy? A bell,
further away than the church
down by the river.

Inside each silence is another
and another, each more complete,
the ones left behind
in the poplars where the town is still remembered.

Wheeze of donkey, washed out blue in a wall.
That's all, that's all, that's all.

I could write books about my father's books.
There was no dust on them. He held them in his hands
as if for the last time. They were quilted,
poised for their moment, shoved in one by one
till they made a smooth wall – one book, all one.

They stole out in golds, in secret reds
as if with a cigarette in the early morning
before the mist has cleared absolutely
into pitilessness. You could touch the titles
and they would be important.

In the dark of them – personal boundaries,
edges he had stepped so close to,
the icy hill over the valley, soldiers clinging
to the slopes, seams of snow,
the Spain he held and held to,
line after line giving way.

RETREAT

So much happened here
just above the village
on that plateau

the one I can't look straight at
mist rising from the cemetery
to it. I have walked all day, looking
to find some shred, tatter,

breath of the unknown, some mercy.
But the plain moves me endlessly on.
I turn round and round in it.

And stop by a row of women
crocheting in front of a house.

Morella, 1938

The rock the town climbs to is warm and worn
and traversed. A farmhouse at the bottom of the hill
its evening lights already in the top right-hand windows.

Daylight weakens where the fields begin.
The fields with their soft enticing earth,
a low band of fire that will appear just before dusk
and then not appear, not be.

The town wall, the stone gates
and the way people gather and keep their voices low
are tried defences. But soon the mayor will be gone.

Word is the retreat has started, they have come,
they enter the town in rags.

LOCAL HISTORY

Here your memory serves you well,
your meticulous study of topography
and human nature.

You can keep a close watch over the hills
and farmlands where day by day,
with the help of maps, you can combine
events – skirmishes, strafing,

with contingencies of weather and light.
You can look through your books,
papers in some quiet. At times
voices from the street reach you,

goodbyes, footsteps that continue.
Certain moments you are studying
also stop in their tracks
like the moment when defeat

first enters the mind and then takes hold.
Write this down, you tell me.
The name of the Mayor was Agustín Borrás Boix.
He was a Republican.

Before he was taken to the cemetery to be shot
he comforted his wife: 'Con el bien que yo he hecho –
las vidas que he salvado –
te parece que me matarán?'*

* *With all the good that I have done –*
the lives I have saved –
do you think they will kill me?

Sardine Tin

I lie down to slide into the shelter
and then stand up in the dark
under the corrugated roof.

It has held all these years
in its line of defence over the Levante
like the crushed gas mask

I find on the slope, the buried
sardine tin. The tin reads 1938,
lid rolled back at a slant, hastily –

like a cape against cold,
or fear or rancour or any emotion that might
break if extended – so thin and expansive

with little rust holes and marks of never.
Up here in the Camarena mountains
the rocks and pine trees are so abundant

and it is my last and only life.
I reach into the tin
with oily fingers I lift to my mouth.

CROSSING AT MIRAVET, 1938

The houses rise up before me unexpectedly.
I can finally see the valley

and the strenuous glimmer that is the Ebro.
A ferry under the poplars, no ferryman.
There is a changing distance to cover.

I listen to the poplars
while I am waiting for the ferry
and look across at the climbed streets

and abandoning houses.
My father sings at the piano.
He closes his eyes.

Al alba venid buen amigo.
Venid a la luz del día.[*]
I am patient till dawn when the soldiers

will enter the Ebro to cross to Miravet
holding their rifles high above the water.

[*] *Come to the dawn good friend.*
Come to the light of day.
        (Spanish song)

Ebro Crossing, 1938

How can I restore them
persistently crossing
over the spilt milk of that river

on pontoon bridges,
in boats or up to their waists in water,
a last hope?

The river – grenade throwers
you walk beside, a mule you ride,
a cannon you pull.

After bombs fall
from the Savoia-Marchettis
there is a soft rushing sound

when earth returns to itself
the smallest particles.
Return, return.

The Mattress

She holds the rolled, striped mattress
on her head and takes long strides

across the plaza so the pigeons start up.
Her boy runs along beside her.

His hair is neatly combed and plastered down –
his coat buttoned. His shoes shine.

She walks firmly across Barcelona
in January 1939.

Military Barracks, Valencia

I focus on getting in
past the swathes of orange
and lemon trees, and by the path
the agave plants dusty and distended,
iron grilles on the windows,
barracks that go round
the block and round again.

What seems to be
when I draw away – a restored calm.
The soldiers who chat in the shade
and smoke. This surface of sanity
and peace. I can't get past it

even though I cross the Turia River
to face it,
even though I feel dread and my mouth is dry.

after a photograph by Robert Capa

Here is a child I know.
He can slip over the border
in his overcoat and blanket.

How can he make a shadow
in these bearing-away hills?
What belongings can he have

here where the trees are so uneasy,
so at a distance?
Wherever I go I see him

along the road from Barcelona.
He is the one I rush back to
in the first light, before anyone is awake,

his bed stripped, the cloistering shutters.
Keep going, keep going I whisper.

> *'A la mar fui por naranjas,*
> *cosa que la mar no tiene.'**
> (Spanish folksong)

They seem to smile in their winter coats
and blankets, suitcases – hundreds of soldiers,
two or three abreast, walking between
the concentration camp at Argelès-sur-Mer
and the concentration camp at Barcarès.
But who can think of even one alone?

They cross those miles of sand in the wind,
with the sand blowing in their eyes
so they must squint which lifts the lips away
from the teeth and gives an enduring, disarmed,
expectant appearance, much as a smile does,
as if this were a passage between two bright

nameless points – the sky silvered over –
or sea resorts, the sand lifting up into the air –
and where it seems to blow towards.

* *'I went to the sea for oranges,*
but the sea has none.'

WHERE DID THEY GO?

Where did they go, the unshakeable ones?
The lost ones, last ones,
wound up in the barrier trees.

After the camps at Argelès-sur-Mer,
St Cyprien, at Barcarès, after the barbed wire
in what places did they choose
or not choose to live, upstairs rooms
so swept by roads and travelling?

I have seen these faces swept across pages,
the stepping forward, the leaning of the body forward
at the border, in the wind. What languages
did they find their timid way among?

What streets did they find to live in,
cities with streets to throng in?

PASSENGER LIST

*'. . . el "Winnipeg", cargado con dos mil republicanos que cantaban y
lloraban, levó anclas y enderezó rumbo a Valparaíso.'*

Pablo Neruda

What I am looking for meets me
among the names: Sánchez,
Martínez, Prado, Gutiérrez, Sáenz.
At the memory of the journey I falter.
It is never so far, if you put one foot
ahead of the other. The shine of the journey
will delay me and noon become night.
Open the porthole. Open the train door.

Is it a poncho I am travelling in?
It will bloom out in the wind of travelling,
red and black, harshly woven.
The journey will take over.
I will be where sand rises in hills
or where the snow line ends.

The face of change will leave me
breathless and alone and give
me courage, forcing the threads down
and the shuttle will hurtle across
the silences of sea and land
tugging at the interminable thread
that is fierce with rays and shoals and ministering fate.

** '. . . the "Winnipeg", laden with two thousand Republicans who sang and wept,
lifted anchor and set sail for Valparaiso.'*

RAIN-STICK

The voice of the cactus slides
backwards, and sliding
inundates me. The voice of these seeds
threads its throat, north to south
trajectory of Chile. Entire cities
rattle down this seedway
where the land is dry and gives fruit
we add sugar and more sugar to.

All night the moon leaves us behind.
The seeds down the causeway shirr
and hardly grip and the pebbles
in the rivers give up their places
reluctantly, torn finally away and down
from the mountains. Nothing can help it,
these seeds in the husk of the cactus
know it is all over
but make the most beautiful
wet sound in transit.

*'Wolle die Wandlung'**
Rainer Maria Rilke

Long before I knew him
he began to get the first letters.
He would glance at the handwriting on the envelopes,
the stamps – he would turn the letters over
as I do, before opening them
by the mailbox that is appearing
and disappearing in the sun,

one from Paris, one from Santiago,
one from Mexico City,
the friends who escaped from Spain
coming to greet him again
under the acacias in Madrid,
standing up to leave him,

what is known and unknown
and the tentativeness he feels now
here, in his new country.
My sister will be born soon.
The birch tree unpeels its bark overhead
ragged paper from its core
and everything that is attends to the living.

* *'Will transformation.'*

When the prisoners returned
from the concentration camps
we spat on them.

When they walked up the hill
and re-entered their streets
where years had passed without them

they were already exhausted
and hopeless, ill, humiliated.
It slides down my face, my shirt.

And I repeat what I did.
I speak slowly and deliberately.

PATERNA 1939-42

I am used to this now.
You can hear the shots as far away
as Burjasot. They are always taken
to the same white wall.

We are all listening
in my fatherless house.

The Northern Lights meet my mother and father.
He has travelled this far to find us all.
My mother imagines his life in Spain
through her love for him. She imagines
streets and barricades, rooms.
In early spring the grass flies straight up
in this bitter wind in New Hampshire.
You can still expect snow and rivers
that bound and are ingenious under the snow.

They run past deep banks and neighbours
in hill farms. The doors close in a consistent
way, bad out, good in. The braided rugs save
from the centre out, made from what is left over,
rags. In thrift they are thrown on the wooden floor
but it's their heat we yearn for, what their twisting
contains. Like the fried churros I dip in hot
chocolate in a winter bar in Zaragoza.

The Northern Lights stream green and yellow,
carmine, they fling down over the meadow.
They rove into the warmest solitude.
They say wherever you settle is fine
as long as you can see us from there.
As long as the changing is insistent.

Not Talking about Franco, 1959

From my uncle's kitchen
I can step out into the courtyard.
I can see way up into the well
of his apartment block
as far as the tiny square of sky

and hang out my clothes
in that heightened Madrid gloom
where the neighbours' clothes
just above drip on them
and sheets and shirts

from many stories up.
I can even hear the tentative
voices from tiled kitchens
just like this one and the leisurely
removal of cutlery, around 3 pm.

The generals are aging.
My uncle pats my hand.
I press his hand.
He smooths the lace tablecloth.

Man O'War

In the war of opposites they are serene, uncanny,
floating, pitching high up on the waves.
These days we can't swim, there are whitecaps
you can see from our porch on the hill,
warnings that flicker even at that distance.

My cousins and I go down to Menemsha
to inspect the jellyfish. They are everywhere –
blue and silver bubbles, their backs sewn and puckered,
and their tendrils mean harm. They come in
after a storm and wind up half dead on the beach.

I look into the bubbles but there is nothing there,
just reflections. I even see the stones through them.
Are they suffering? The wind dies at my feet.
But when they are out at sea
they seem to carry the blue, entering days to us

willing the beginning of change
when they ride in so helplessly and fiercely.

COASTLINE, 1960

When you see your country for the first time again
from another country,
turn back to the café tables and conversation.

Your brother and sister have come from Madrid
and Las Palmas to meet you here in Tangiers.
They have grandchildren now.

There are colonies of seaweed, bottles,
fast boats come from there, swinging
and altering between the two coasts.

It is just over the water, the pace of Spain
– a long line, an interminable line
you walk on every day without stopping

in your suit and tie, holding your hat –
when you want to go inland
away from the depths of your resolve

those days when the air is clear and fine.

Today I met you, son of a Spanish exile
in a London café, far from Mexico
where you grew up, I far from my native New York.
We talked about our fathers.
Both died before Franco died.
Neither returned to Spain.

When you told me your father's story
we were in that invisible cage
I imagine the children of exiles live in,
open to wind and night.
My eyes filled with tears

and the wires of the cage lit up for a moment
so all those photographs I had seen
became moving people, breathing,
heavy with rain, suitcases, blankets,
warm with their pasts still inside them

pressing against the wires of the cage
that war and our fathers made for us.
Enter, we said, Enter, welcome.

ELOUNDA, CRETE, 1966

That evening, on the salt flats
a man and a donkey went all the way out
to the end of the promontory.
My hands and face were smudged with salt.

A good house
took us in, all garden and whitewash
and the horizon showed through
like my arm through a frayed sleeve.
This was almost Spain for my father,
as near as he would get, anyway.

I wanted to see how far the man and the donkey
would go before they stopped
how dark it would get, without hope

the repetitive slow journey along that narrow strip
salt crystallising even on my lips
in the expectant heat, stone barriers
criss-crossing the bay, calm

how you can live
your whole life in one place, just one.

I borrowed a brush from a nearby grave.
The briars grew high around yours –
and the burrs stuck to my dress.
When I swept away the dust and water
flakes of whitewash dislodged.
I enjoyed the movement of the brush
and that I was doing, after all, something practical
that you would have liked,
pushing the long water across your grave.
In the corners the clean pools shone –
a feeling of ease and custom, as if I had walked
round and round the grave with smoking
incense as I have seen daughters do in Crete –
lighting the oil lamp in a glass case
that has a cigarette packet, a photograph,
busying themselves, laying down fresh basil.

THE WAREHOUSE, 1998

They bring their chairs here every day —
plastic chairs they can carry easily or drag
and line up in front of a warehouse door.
From here they can see, because of the twists
and turns of the town in its rapid descent
right over the hills and mountains

and as far out as the horizon
where no day lasts or holds steady.
They can see where the battlefield was
and they can load their old age, their poor eyesight,
with the barriers of mountains they could hardly
imagine climbing now. There is a ridge of shade

along the warehouse door, never mind
the heat, and they sit in this, in a row and talk.
They are so old now, a little younger
than my father would be if he had lived.
They all fought in the Civil War.
But I don't ask which side they were on

or who they lost, who betrayed them,
what forced them to join which cause.
It is all so long ago now.
Here in this sunlight, this silence
they rest in and break, and welcome me to.